Pain into POWER

Pain into **POWER**

There's Beauty on the Other Side of Pain

Briya Brown

Published by Pain to Powerhouse, LLC.

Book Formatting by Derek Murphy @Creativindie

Pain Into Power : There's Beauty on the Other Side of Pain

Copyright © 2021 by Briya Brown.

All rights reserved. Printed in the United States of America. No part of this book may be used or reproduced in whole or in part, in any form or by any means, electronic or mechanical, including photocopying, recording, or by any information storage and retrieval system now known or hereafter invented, without written permission from the publisher.

Visit us on the web at :

www.paintopowerbook.com

Book Cover Design by Anneisha Finney

ISBN: 978-0-578-89514-7

DEDICATION

"We don't know ourselves by what we get right; we know ourselves by what we get wrong"

– Suzanne Stabile

The Road Back To You: An Enneagram Journey To Self-Discovery

This book is dedicated to everyone I've experienced, good and bad, who have shaped me to be the woman I am today. Thank you.

CONTENTS

Introduction 1
Part I: Who Am I? 9
   I: Self-Made 11
Part II: The Pressing 25
   II: Reflection 27
   III: Stop Having Sex 35
   IV: Staying Beyond the Expiration Date 41
   V: Red Flags are Deal Breakers 47
   VI: Listen to Your Gut 53
   VII: If You Focus on The Package, You'll Miss The Gift 57
   VIII: Trust Has to Be Earned 64
   IX: Stop Trying to Figure It Out 71
   X: You Can't Change People 77
   XI: Love Yourself More 82
   XII: Don't Settle 87
   XIII: Invest in Yourself 93

Part III: Growth 97
   XIV: God 99
   XV: Forgive Yourself 105
   XVI: Heal 109
   XVII: Master Your Emotions 115
   XVIII: Boundaries 120
   XIX: Relationships 124
Part IV: Briya 2.0 131
   XX: A Legacy of Love 133
About the Author 136
Acknowledgments 137

INTRODUCTION

"Experience is the teacher of all things"
—*De Bello Civili*

It's December 24, 2020, Christmas Eve, and during a global pandemic. We've been quarantined for about nine months now and I am not able to be with my family during the Christmas and New Year holiday. I just found out a dear friend of mine decided to end our friendship with no explanation. I reached out and nothing. Two days prior, December 22, 2020, I had a falling out with a guy I had recently began getting to know for about two and a half months. Ultimately, I found out he wasn't who he said he was and it really broke my spirit. I'm confused, I'm hurt, I'm stressed, and I just don't know what to do anymore. I am alone in my apartment crying my eyes out on the phone with my mother and ask, "Is it me? Am I bad person? I just don't understand." She replies, "No, Briya. You're not.

You cannot control what other people do. If you try to fight every battle, you're going to be worn the hell out."

In that moment, I realized she was right. She always has been. Have you ever been tired of your own shit? Have you ever found yourself making the same mistakes and finding yourself in the same trauma patterns? Have you ever wanted to do better and want better for yourself but it just doesn't seem to be happening? Have you ever thought you learned a lesson just to find yourself in the same cycle?

Do you know who you are? Do you know why you do the things you do? Do you have traumas? Insecurities? Are you healing? These are all of the questions that are rushing through my head as I'm trying to decipher how and why life is coming down so hard on me in the span of two days. It also has me reflecting on everything that has happened in my life, where I am in life, where I want to be, and who I want to be.

I'm about to start my last semester in law school in a few weeks and prepare for this next big chapter in my life. I should feel excited, be happy and ecstatic. Yet, once again, I've let the woes of life weigh me down. I've just experienced another painful situation and I'm back in the cycle of trying to make meaning of it. I'm beating myself up about what I could've done and worrying about what people think and constantly feeling the need to prove and defend myself. I'VE HAD ENOUGH.

I started my journey of intentional self-development and healing at the beginning of the pandemic (March 2020), but I was still making mistakes and finding myself in repetitive cycles. Believe it or not, Christmas Eve I experienced an awakening. It was that moment that I knew I would look back when I'm much older and will say, "I was 26 when I finally got it." Not to say that I've reached my ultimate growth peak and there's nothing else to learn. I just mean this is my awakening. I've been in a constant period of reflection. Life truly has a way of teaching you things. Experience is the best teacher.

But before you read any further, let me tell you what this book is not. Some will say experience is not always the best teacher. Experience does often times produce wisdom, but for some, it also produces bitterness, fear and cynicism. A lot of people learn the wrong things from negative situations whether it be relationship failures, employee-employer issues, business partnerships and more. The most common is relationship failures and that entails all types of relationships—

platonic, familial and romantic. From these experiences, many people learn, just like myself, not to trust, not to care too much, not to invest too much of oneself, not to have high expectations, and the list goes on.

This list is perfect for guarding, protecting, and maintaining a heart of steel. It's even perfect to avoid pain, loss and failure. However, these are precisely the wrong behaviors to embody for building long-lasting, vibrant relationships of all types. No relationship will thrive without trust, commitment, and vulnerability. That is not what this book is. I am not saying that the only way to learn about relationships and how to navigate life is through mistakes and negative experiences. I am not saying that we must endure failure and pain in order to learn and mature. We learn from both positive and negative experiences.

The point of this book is to say that the real teacher is not the experiences themselves, but the reflection and self-introspection and retrospection that should accompany them to be a better you and navigate this thing called life. After sitting with myself for so long, I realized the truth is experience, both positive and negative, only really help us if we take the time to reflect on it. Taking that time for yourself, you in turn will extract the right lessons from it and as a result change your behavior, attitude and perspective in a positive way. In order to be effective in this process, you have to reflect on both the intrinsic and extrinsic factors.

Intrinsic factors include the internal aspects within oneself: character and personality flaws, emotions, how we react to an external stressor, and destructive attitudes and habits. Extrinsic factors are ones that exert their influence from the outside and most of the time are not in our control. That can be personality flaws in other people, unfortunate events in life, illnesses, etc. Effective reflection is key. Let me tell you why. Most people, just like myself, spend so much time justifying our grievances, victimizing and placing blame for our hurt and pain that often times we ignore the vitally important intrinsic factors that played a role and we have control over.

It's interesting. Many people look at me and my successes, my life, my image on social media and assume that I have it all figured out. I get so many messages from people telling me how much of an inspiration I am, how strong I am, how dedicated I am, how hardworking I am, how resilient I am. That's always been my aspiration in life. I want to inspire people. I want to inspire people to be better, to do better, to do the things they've been programmed to believe they can't do or are not meant for them. Most of the time, those messages come with a comparison relative to themselves.

Whenever I get those type of messages, I make sure to be transparent about where I am in life, what I struggle with and what I've gone through. Like most individuals, I only show people what I want them to see. In this period of heightened social media use where everybody's life is a highlight reel, it's important to acknowledge that that is unrealistic. I too struggle. Sometimes I fall short. Man, I can't tell you how many days and nights I've cried. There have been times I felt like I just couldn't do it anymore and wanted to give up. There are times I am not disciplined. And sometimes I am the problem.

Nonetheless, whether it's your own experience or someone else's, learning from experience is just a useless exercise if it doesn't translate into a change in behavior. It doesn't matter whether the experience was a negative one or the best thing to ever happen to you. If we do not reflect properly, experience won't teach you anything, or worse, teach you the wrong things. This isn't about getting the revenge body to show that guy what he missed out on. This isn't about bossing up to show your former business partner because they betrayed you. This is about you. Do it for *you*. You owe it to yourself and no one else.

So, this is for me. Writing this book has been so therapeutic and enlightening for me. I've owed this to myself for so long and I know this will help so many people. I've always told people, "One day I'm going to write a book about my story." So, here it is.

PART I

WHO AM I?

1

SELF-MADE

"Your legacy is being written by yourself. Make the right decisions."
—Gary Vaynerchuk

You see the title of this chapter. "Self-made". According to my Google search, "self-made" is a term that was coined by Henry Clay in the United States Senate to describe individuals whose success lay within the individuals themselves, not with outside conditions. When most people hear self-made, what follows behind that is some billionaire who's made it big. For example, my Google search also tells me that Jeff Bezos, Amazon founder with a current net worth of more than $155 billion, is one of the richest self-made men there is.

Pain Into Power

No, I am not a billionaire (yet, God willing). I am not a Bill Gates or a Warren Buffett. I am, however, Briya Brown. I am a 26-year-old, young Black woman entrepreneur, graduating law school, now an author, who has managed to occupy spaces not intended for me, in a system designed against my favor. While I am not the only young Black woman to achieve this, it is definitely a different level of self-made.

To start, I'll tell you a little bit about myself and how I got here. Growing up as a Prince George's County, Maryland native, I grew up under the single mother narrative. My parents divorced when I was really young but my father was always in the picture. I mainly lived with my mother and watched her be a superwoman all of my life, even until this very day. I watched her work multiple jobs to make sure my brother and I wanted for nothing. She would wake up at 5AM and not return home until almost 10PM and she's been doing this all of her life. I've watched my mom give us her last while she had nothing. I've watched my mother make something out of nothing. Everyday.

The crazy part about it is, she never complained once. My mother is the reason I am the woman I am today. She pushed me and stayed on my tail my entire life. I remember bringing my grades home to show her and she would say, "Those Bs are good but you have to do better". This is why many people described me as the overachiever growing up. Honestly, I am glad my mother raised me in that manner or else I may have become a "settle for anything" type of woman. You know, the "Cs get degrees" mentality. While that is true, this mindset fosters a lazy mentality, work-ethic and attitude. In my mother's household, Cs were not acceptable and had I brought one home...oh boy. I truly aspire to be the woman my mother is someday. She is truly a phenomenal woman.

So, I have three siblings, two brothers and a sister, and I am the youngest. I don't have a close relationship with any of them for various reasons. To protect the privacy of my family, those reasons I will not disclose. Because of that, I've pretty much grown up as an only child, or at least it has felt that way. I was the golden child. I didn't really get into much trouble, I did what I was told, graduated high school and went to college. I excelled in school at every level. Because of this, the pressure was always on me. I felt the need to always be perfect or I'd be a failure to my parents. Because I was the only one doing things right, the focus on me made me very cautious and particular about what I did.

I went to Salisbury University for my undergraduate studies where I received a dual-degree in Political Science and Spanish, with a minor in Latin American Studies. In fact, middle school was where my aspiration to become a lawyer was rooted. My best friend from middle school inspired this passion that I have today. I grew up with her and her family for a few years. We attended school together and afterwards I would always stay at her house. Her mother would cook us lunch and dinner, I would play with her and her sisters, and sometimes I even tagged along with her while she *had* to do things that I wasn't used to...things I *didn't have to do*.

This is when I knew I wanted to be a lawyer. We were in middle school and only about ten years old. My friend and her family were from Mexico. Then, I didn't know her story or even what it meant. I just remember all of her family living in that house were the hardest working people ever and my friend had a lot of adult responsibilities. We had time to do children activities, but a lot of that time was cut short due to her having to watch her younger sisters, or walk to the grocery store to get groceries for her family, or make important phone calls because she was the only one who really understood and could speak fluent English.

Back then, I didn't really understand the logistics of it all. I just knew I wanted to help. I could relate to her and her family in a way. We both were part of disadvantaged communities, both distinct, but still similar in many ways. And from there on out, I knew that was my calling. You can ask pretty much anyone. I was telling everyone that I wanted to be a lawyer at a young age. And here I am, less than five months away from graduating law school.

So, upon graduating from Salisbury University, I had a plan. I was going to start law school immediately after and have this and that done by this and that age. I was wrong. Life happened and my plans did not go how I expected them to play out. I took two years in between undergraduate school to gain work experience in the legal field and to begin studying for the LSAT. In those two years, life happened again and that experience empowered me to start my own business, Body By Bri, LLC.

I developed a passion for health and fitness during undergraduate school. If you knew me then, I was always in the gym. After graduating and taking my first steps into the real world, I began to see real world issues. My college problems were nothing compared to these problems. When people say "enjoy your time in college because the real world is not a joke", listen. They mean it. And, they were right. However, there was one problem that became clear to me that I knew I wanted to be part of the solution. That was the health disparities in the Black community.

Not only just the Black community, but all vulnerable communities. That is why I started Body By Bri, LLC. Body By Bri, LLC is a health and fitness brand that was founded in November of 2017. Body By Bri, LLC was created for the purpose of helping vulnerable communities by combating health disparities and structural inequalities in the health and wellness industry. The goal is to help these communities adopt and maintain healthier lifestyles. My business embodies self-love, authenticity and empowerment. By starting this business, I made it my social obligation to advocate and inspire people to prioritize their health now, so that they won't be forced to make time for their illness later.

African-Americans, along with other minority communities, experience significant disparities with chronic conditions, access to healthcare and resources, mental health and preventative screenings. For me, what I noticed was the alarming fact that in almost every low-income/poor community, there is a McDonald's on every block. When confronted with very limited budgets, families are more inclined to purchase food based on cost rather than nutritional value. Unfortunately, we all know a fresh salad can costs around $10 to $20 while an entree of a burger, fries and a soda can cost as low as $4. This, coupled with sedentary lifestyles and health destructive habits, is the silent killer among us. Our culture and respective upbringing have a significant influence on our lifestyle choices.

Growing up, my family would gather together almost every Sunday and eat soul food and drink sodas and alcohol (You know, all of the works. Fried chicken, potato salad, macaroni and cheese, candied yams, stuffing, grilled chicken, chitlings, tuna salad, chicken salad, fried fish, rolls, collard greens, green beans and more). Some of it may not sound bad but trust me. These dishes are made with nothing but loads of salt, sugar, butter and grease. It was so bad that the people in my family who tried to do and eat better are laughed at. If someone brings a salad or vegetarian options, everyone is like, "Who brought salad? Nobody wants that". Not only did my family have horrible nutritional habits, I noticed that majority of them also had sedentary lifestyles and regularly engaged in activities such as smoking and drinking.

My grandmother passed away at 75 on May 11, 2019, the day before Mother's Day. Her passing was due to having a number of conditions and diseases, all associated with her nutrition and lack of movement. Diseases such as diabetes and high blood pressure run rampant in minority communities. Because I know of the issues that sometimes prevent these communities from being able to take control of their health and because we don't see a lot of people that look like me in the fitness industry, I decided to create that safe space and offer affordable and accessible services.

I offer personal training services, group exercise classes, meal preparations, freshly pressed juices, online programs, preventative screenings, athletic apparel and accessories. This journey in the fitness industry has led me to be featured on 93.9 WKYS's "Millennial Money Moves" and earning a spot on the Seagrams Escape Holiday Marketplace featuring Black-Owned Businesses, a partnership with Cnythia Bailey and Eva Marcille. So, instead of watching my family and others continue to make detrimental lifestyle choices, I decided to hold myself and everyone around me accountable for their lives.

Then, it's June of 2018. I found out I was admitted into law school after what seemed to be a long struggle to get there. In my head, all I could think was I made it. My parents will be so proud. I am one step closer to my dreams becoming my reality. So, fast forward to today. I am currently a third-year law student at the University of Baltimore School of Law. I am less than five months away from graduating and I couldn't be more excited. I started law school as a part-time evening student while working a full-time job at the Baltimore City State's Attorney's Office as a law clerk in the Special Victims Unit.

On this track, I was set to graduate law school in May of 2022. However, I decided that I wanted to graduate in the typical three years and now I'm doing just that. While still working a full-time job and being a full-time entreprenuer, I took consecutive semesters from Fall of 2018 up until this final semester, Spring of 2021. I hustled through Fall, Winter, Spring and Summer classes non-stop for three years. I never had a break. While in law school, I became very involved. I was so involved that I have to dedicate an entire paragraph to tell you.

I served as President and Vice President of the Immigration Law Association. I prepared academic resources, opportunities for professional development, and community outreach. During my time in these positions, I made pro bono service a foundation of the organization as well as an obligation as part of our community social responsibility. I have volunteered with immigration attorneys to help eligible permanent residents apply for citizenship. I attended the sixth annual Refugee/Asylee Green Card Clinic where I helped assist refugees and asylees with the adjustment of status ("green card") applications. I also coordinated my own immigration clinic dedicated to giving back to the community—a partnership with the Kennedy Kreiger Center and screened their patients for possible immigration options.

I also served as part of the Access to Justice Commission's student committee. The Access to Justice Commission is a collaborative entity that brings together courts, the bar, civil legal aid providers, and other stakeholders in an effort to remove barriers to civil justice for low-income and disadvantaged people.[1] I also served as the Evening Representative of the Student Bar Association and a Student Committee member of the

---

[1] https://www.mdaccesstojustice.org/

Student Bar Association Mental Health Program dedicated to improving and finding solutions to help law students improve their mental health and cope with stress.

In this organization, I organized and facilitated a sound healing meditation session for the student body to introduce a new form of therapy. I also served as the Community Service Chair for the Latin American Law Students Association where I was responsible for seeking out and organizing monthly community service opportunities for our members. Finally, I currently serve as a BarBri representative (a Bar preparation company) and as a Student Representative for the Alliance of Black Women Attorneys. *Whew, I know.*

So, I know you're probably thinking, her life sounds great. As I told you before, I lived a pretty privileged life and I've never really wanted for much. And because I was the golden child, I feared so much of making mistakes and doing the wrong thing that I spent every day trying to live up to that image. However, and that's a big HOWEVER, the only issues I have had are the ones that have motivated me to write this book. It's why you're here. It's the *only* thing that has stressed my parents out to death about me. It is the only thing that I've been ashamed of for so long and has made me feel like I've disappointed my parents. It's the only thing that has been able to derail me from my plans and make me lose myself a number of times.

It is the only thing that has made me want to give up on life and have almost lost it *all*. That thing....is love. They do say experience is the best teacher, right? Well, the one thing that has broken me down time after time, is the same thing that has made me a better me. It's the same thing that has shaped me into the woman I am today and still becoming. It's the same thing that has taught me the most about myself. It's the same thing that has taught me the most about life. It's the one thing that has caused the most havoc and pain in my life. But each time, I came out better and stronger.

Someone recently told me that my story reminds them of the Phoenix. If you don't know what the Phoenix is, I'll give you some insight. In ancient mythology, the symbolism of the majestic Phoenix bird, which is most often connected with the Sun, dies by bursting into flames and is reborn. It is reborn from the ashes to start a new, long life. The Phoenix bird symbolizes birth, death, and resurrection as well as eternity, strength and renewal.

The whole idea that this mythical bird is reborn from the ashes of the flames of death signifies a journey through fire or adversity.[2] And that is what this book is about. How I turned my pain into power. How that pain was the most transformative for my life. Not only did I rise from the ashes not smelling like smoke, I became a better person. A better me. There really is beauty on the other side of pain.

---

2   Symbolism of the Mythical Phoenix Bird: Renewal, Rebirth, and Destruction, Myth Legends. www.ancient-origins.net

PART II

THE PRESSING

The pressing represents an all-encompassing journey—the spiritual, mental, emotional and physical—during the most trying times of life. It's similar to the process of grapes being crushed in order to be turned into wine. The pressing isn't meant to break you, it's meant to preserve you.

II

REFLECTION

"Trust your ability to learn and grow from every experience, be it good or bad. In any circumstance that comes your way, use it to make yourself a better person."

— *Rob Hill Sr*

Remember when I said earlier that if we do not reflect properly, experience either will not teach you anything or will teach you the wrong things? Right. Well, in my experience, it took me a while to realize that. I kept finding myself in the same situations and making the same mistakes and never really reflecting on them. Just moving onto the next one. I found myself in one of the top three most horrific situations that made me realize I really need to sit with myself and reflect on these situations. As I said before, this journey of reflection, healing and self-development started in March 2020.

However, during this process, I *still* found myself sticking my foot into situations I should've never been able to find had I been intentional. That is what I mean by reflection needs to be done properly. Before, I would meditate, journal, pray, and study the word of God until the next situation presented itself to me and then all of sudden, the process went out the window because I thought I had it all down. I was good. I thought I learned the lesson and thought I was okay. I was strong. I could handle this. Wrong. Wrong. *Wrong*.

So, instead of me going on and on in detail about the specific situations that happened to me (which I could write a book about on its own), these following chapters will be the lessons extracted from those experiences after proper reflection. These are lessons that we all need to master. I used to be told so many times, "it's because you are young" or "it's different, we're older". But the truth is, many adults in their 40s and even 50s are struggling with the very same issues. I'm just glad that it didn't take me until 40 to realize these things.

Before I dive into the most imperative lessons that, if you haven't yet learned, will change your life, attitude and behavior, I want to share one of the first letters I wrote during one of my moments of stillness. I remember this day. I was sad, I tried meditating, used my sound bowls, stretched, prayed, and just sat with my feelings. I cried and then I opened my computer and wrote a letter titled, "A letter to my last, both past and future". This was a letter addressed to my last, my ex-boyfriend, as an acknowledgement of my faults and in the same addressed to my last, being my future husband, as an acknowledgment of my growth and how I'm actively working on my past traumas and healing so that I will get it right with him. It read:

"A letter to my last...both past and future....
I had to look at myself and be honest.

The main lesson in this moment of stillness is "Adversity is not meant to steal from you or destroy you, but help you find you...help you find the giant within." Life is not the enemy.

*When I'm hurt- my first reaction is to reciprocate that hurt, defend, blame.......**victimize.***

Throughout my healing process I have learned (and still learning) to calm and quiet the fighter, *even through the biggest hurt and the deepest cut, and just sit with that pain with an **open heart**. Walk with openness but also with a realization that there is no ground underneath me. BUT understanding that the ground under my feet is of a higher power.*

*My view on religion/spirituality is that there exists a higher power and each man has their own interpretation of who and what that higher power is. During this stillness, I am taking the time to **cultivate** my relationship with that higher power. In this stillness, as I maintain discipline and trust, I have seen the beauty and the depth of love that pours from this relationship and it always meets me with an embrace. It has helped me understand and see what I need to change within and what trauma pattern that I am in.*

I've learned that you can't ask for signs without intention. Instead of crying why is this happening to me, during my stillness I ask why am I feeling this pain, where is this coming from...The universe always answers.

It was never about you or what you did to me... the things you did to me. When the inevitable happens—hurt—it's always been something is wrong with me or something is wrong with you, but either way something is wrong. During this stillness, I've learned that I've been wrong. **It was never about you or what you did to me...the things you did to me.** *I now ask myself, "What is this showing me about myself?" No matter what happens, I have to take responsibility. I can no longer hold onto blame or victim. I let this situation into my life, so why? At the end of the day, that is what I have to look at because that is the only thing that I have control over. Looking at how I'm relating to people, how I'm being affected, how I'm affecting others, but most importantly, only looking at* **MY part***. That is a high level of responsibility and it has been hard. It has revealed why I'm making the decisions I've made and why I'm letting certain dynamics and people into my life. "Nobody can do unto you what you don't allow."*

If I am not willing to take responsibility, my life will not change. I will be stuck in certain patterns if I am not willing to look at myself.

This is a hard process because you have to accept the shadows. Love them as they leave. Aversion and attachment. Self-care isn't telling myself, "You're a bad bitch". It's looking at your demons and your past, sitting and being patient with myself. There are real powerful blessings on the other side of pain.

I want to attract an honest person. Therefore, I need to be ready to receive that honesty. No hiding and no harboring. I don't want to spend a lifetime *figuring out how to not be found out. Masking. The idea of romanticism tells us that love is red. Overly passionate, aggressive, barely containable, heart pounding, and burning desire. I've learned that love is actually **blue**. It's calm...it's **peaceful**. It stills your heart and it is the shelter. It isn't perfect, nothing is perfect, but it's built on a solid foundation of respect and kindness. I need honesty upfront about who you are and your struggles. And if you feel like you can't open up about that right away, I want to create a **safe space** for you to do so. I believe that love **should** feel like a safe space and is most pure when it is offered **purposefully**, expressed from a place of sound mind and **intentional** heart.*

*I've learned that I am not the only the one hurting. Therefore, when I think about who it is I want to be? What kind of life do I want?... I want to lead with love and leave a legacy of love. Love is compassionate, it is not unkind, it is not romanticism, it's not always easy, it is not cruel, and ego has **no** place."*

And there you have it. I know. The feels. Take it all in. This is the first and most important lesson because all the other lessons you will learn and new habits and behaviors you will adopt, will come from the act of proper reflection. Believe it or not, I wrote this letter with tears in my eyes.

Healing isn't always pretty, just like self-care isn't always a hot bath and face masks. Sometimes self-care is doing the very things we don't want to do but know we need to do (i.e., letting go of a relationship, ending a friendship, leaving that job).

In this case, it's sitting with yourself, your emotions and your feelings. Feeling painful emotions, not surprisingly, can be painful. This is why so many people don't do it. Instead, we ignore our emotions and attempt to numb them with alcohol, drugs, sex, retail therapy, another relationship or whatever your escape may be. We basically turn to anything that will help us forget about how we feel.

This time was different. I wanted better for myself so I decided to actually sit still and unpack my experiences. Ray Dalio, the author of *Principles*, argues that pain "is a signal that you need to find solutions so you can progress."[3] Only by exploring it and reflecting on it can we start to learn and evolve. Sitting with your emotions simply means just allowing them to be, resisting the urge to get rid of the pain and not judging yourself for experiencing those emotions. Majority of the time, when most people are done with a relationship or just experienced loss or failure, we

---

3 *Principles: Life and Work*, Ray Dalio; September 2017

rarely take the time to reflect on what was really the problem. We often think of the fight but not the underlying cause. And if we do think of the cause, it always the fault of another person or something other than ourself.

Try very hard not to do that. I know it's easy to place blame. It feels better to have someone to blame for our feelings and why we're hurt. But, I challenge you to try something new. Don't rush through the pain or avoid it. Stay in it, sit with it, get to know it and explore it so you can foster improvement. And to put it in perspective, I'd like to echo Ray Dalio in that "it is really why confession precedes forgiveness in many societies."[4] If you make reflection a habit when you encounter trying times—remember, proper reflection—then you will begin to transform your pain, mess and weaknesses into something powerful and purposeful. That's the beauty on the other side of pain.

---

4   Ray Dalio

STOP HAVING SEX

"Discernment is the ability to see things for what they really are and not what you want them to be."

—*Unknown*

Stop. Having. Sex. I know that might sound like a lot for some, but really. Stop it. If you are single, I encourage you to abstain from sex in a way that's seemingly not religious or, if you're a believer, abstain with purpose. Abstinence and celibacy are usually terms that are used interchangeably, however, they are not the same. Abstinence is the choice and practice of simply not having sex. Celibacy often has religious connotations, where an individual or couple decides not to partake in sexual activity in order to strengthen their relationship with God. While I would encourage the latter, it doesn't matter which one you decide to practice. Just stop having sex. I'm going to tell you why.

My mother would ALWAYS tell me "sex just complicates things" and I would always have some rebuttal as to how sex had nothing to do with any of the issues I was experiencing. After reflecting, she was right...again. I know she's going to read this and smile and say, "I told you." But sex really does complicate things. I know you're probably thinking, "no it doesn't", "we're adults", "sex is just sex". No. It is so much deeper than that. Here are my reasons and rationale for abstaining from sex:

1. **Date with Clear Eyes**
   When you're abstaining from sex while dating, you're able to date and see with clear eyes. By clear eyes, I mean you gain discernment. It's much easier to weed out who is not meant for you when you abstain from sex. It also helps you to really learn what people's intentions are with you. People can and will say one thing, but trust and believe, the real intentions will come out to light. You're also not giving yourself up and giving your body to any and everyone. The First Law of Thermodynamics states

that energy cannot be created or destroyed, but can be transformed or transferred. Sexual energy is real. When you are abstaining from sex, you're not exchanging sexual energies and taking on what comes along with that. That allows you to be able to discern what is good and what is not good for you.

2. **Attachments**

This is really where that "sex just complicates things" comes into play. The reality is that sex does create attachments. Unfortunately, if the attachment is created with the wrong person, the unhealthy attachment, this can result in so many things. Attachments prevent you from having that discernment we just talked about. Instead of doing what's best for you and standing true to what you know you deserve, you start to make excuses and find reasons to stay in a place you don't belong. I've been so attached to the wrong person in the past where it drove me crazy. Unhealthy attachments have tainted how I see myself. I remember feeling and thinking, "how will I ever move on?", "I'm never going to find someone like you", "I can't be without you". All false and unhealthy behaviors that attachments cause when you are not with the right person.

3. **Self-Control/Discipline**
   One thing that you will absolutely gain from abstaining from sex is self-control. If you struggle with being discipline in certain areas of your life, this will be the one area of your life that will be the foundation to this new found discipline. It will create a snowball effect into other areas of your life where you lack. That can be going to the gym and prioritizing your health or it could be over indulging on food. When you master that self-control, you will no longer engage with things or people that you know are not good for you. Let me repeat that again. This is important because a lot of us are entertaining, engaging and keeping things and/or people in our lives while knowing they are not good for us. The mastery of self-control deters you from engaging with things and people that are not good for you. In actuality, practicing self-control and discipline will actually start to attract things that are meant for you and beneficial to your life.

4. **Know Your Worth – Self Discovery**
   Another benefit of this journey is that you will gain self-worth. Actually, you'll know your worth and then add tax. Abstinence is

also good for personal maturation. You gain a stronger sense of your worth and who you are. You're not that person who has that tainted view of themselves anymore. It's no more, "I'm so hurt", "I'm broken", "I'm not loveable", or whatever the sentiment may be. You achieve an ultimate level of self-awareness to the point that you're so rooted in you that nothing or no one can shake you and you will accept nothing less than what you want and know you deserve. Period.

5. **Peace of Mind**
Having peace of mind is one of the key ingredients to personal happiness and development. One thing that disrupts one's peace of mind is fear and worry, which for me at least, often comes with being sexually active and intimate with others. Fear of diseases, worrying about not being the only one, fear of the potential consequences of not being the only one, why is he/she doing that, why won't they change, and all that jazz. Abstinence will provide complete freedom from these worries.

6. **Sexually Transmitted Diseases and Unplanned Pregnancies (The Obvious)**
   This one is self-explanatory and therefore there's no need to elaborate on this. Just know that one mistake can lead to a lifetime change or something that can't be fixed.

IV

STAYING BEYOND THE EXPIRATION DATE

"Knowing when to walk away is wisdom. Being able to is courage. Walking away with your head held high is dignity."

—*Unknown*

I, along with many people, date with the intention and ultimate goal of finding a life partner and getting married. However, when the current relationship isn't working out or meeting your needs and expectations, the smart thing to do would be to end the relationship. I'm not ashamed to say this, but I have not always done the smart thing to do. I have remained in relationships and situations with expiration dates for various reasons: having unhealthy attachments, what I thought was "love", not wanting to be alone, not wanting to start over, or just holding onto potential. With this lesson, you HAVE to understand that although everyone comes into your life for a reason, that reason may not be a lifelong reason. It could be that they were meant to teach you a lesson and only here for a season.

Sometimes knowing when to stay and when to go can be complicated. A lot of the times it's a battle between your heart and your mind. Whether it's a family member, friend, romantic partner, or co-worker, the people in your life can either add to your life or take away from it. The big struggle is usually choosing to stay in a relationship where there's been emotional pain and conflict, but you continue to hold onto how it used to be or what you hope for it to become.

Then, there's the staying in a conflict-filled relationship with the hope and wonder if it will strengthen the bond. You know, those romanticized toxic relationships. The ride or dies. The ones that insinuate that you must endure cheating, dishonesty, pain and suffering to get to that end goal of a solid, strengthened relationship. However, neither of these will result in a positive outcome. I've learned five important ideas to consider when it's time to check the expiration date:

1. **Sound Decisions**
   Make sure you are making a decision with a sound mind. This means that you shouldn't make decisions when you're upset or angry. When we are emotional, we tend to make impulsive decisions based on how we are feeling in the moment rather than actually considering all things relevant. We sometimes end friendships under emotional states like this, only to realize that the relationship has value and has more positives than negatives. I've also made bad decisions based on my mental state at the time. There have been times where I may have entertained someone or allowed someone in my life just a little longer because I liked the attention or wasn't ready yet to be alone. When you are emotional, it's hard to be calm and think with a sound and wise mind. Problem solving becomes difficult. Breathe and take a step back.

2. **Pros and Cons**
   Make a pro and con list of that person in your life so that you can determine the reasons a

relationship may need to end. It's one thing to turn a blind eye to certain things or behavior, but to see it written down in a pros and cons list really brings things into perspective. You will see that con list and think "what am I doing?". But don't slip into the habit of justifying the cons. "Well, she's healing so it'll take time" or "Well, he only did it twice and he's learned the lesson." A list like this helps you see the overall picture more clearly.

3. **Give and Take**
   Consider the give and take. Determine whether the relationship enhances your life or is destructive, restrictive and limiting. Remember that love is not always enough. People in your life should inspire you to be better in all aspects. They should encourage, support and uplift you. But also remember this, sometimes in those relationships—whether it's familial, romantic, or platonic—there may be times when you have to give 80% while the other can only give 20%. There is a thin line with this and it's imperative to first know is this person supposed to be in your life, are they in alignment and fruitful to your life.

4. **Who you are in this relationship**
   Look at what it brings out in you. Does this relationship bring the best you out? Or are you becoming someone you don't like? Are you doing things that aren't like yourself? The dynamics of a relationship that is not meant for you will bring out all types of personal dysfunction, nastiness and a foreign version of yourself to the extent that you will no longer be able to recognize you.

5. **Alignment**
   Alignment. Alignment. Alignment. Are you guys aligned? Do you see eye to eye? Are you on the same page? Are you always in a state of conflict and arguing? Alignment within a relationship means that you are loving and living in the same direction as someone else. If you don't take the time and effort to make sure you're align with their vision, goals, core values and passions, it will show in the relationship. For me, dating people not in alignment with my values, standards, goals and vision looked like dating a man who didn't believe in God. It looked like dating a man who had a child, wasn't ready for a relationship, baby mama issues and more. Maintain tunnel vision when it comes to your values, morals, standards

desires, goals and vision. When you steer away from that, it goes from being aligned to being all over the place.

Honestly, the best way to start unpacking all of this is by trying to see things more objectively. Without taking a step back you could find yourself doing something you later regret because you didn't know which way to turn or kept going when you should've stopped. Whatever you do decide, remember that the decision about whether or not to continue with your relationship is one you make. You shouldn't worry about what other people think, or what you think you're *supposed* to do. Do what's best for you, even if it hurts. Pain is temporary.

V

RED FLAGS ARE DEAL BREAKERS

"Ignoring the signs is a good way to end up in the wrong destination."

—Unknown

This is one of the lessons I struggled with the most. Red flags are not red flags. They're actually deal breakers. Let me use the visual of an alarm clock. Our alarms make loud noise to signal that it is time to wake up. If you're anything like me, you probably will hit the snooze button or sometimes you don't hear it all and you sleep through the alarm. What happens when you continue to snooze or sleep through the alarm? You're waking up late and rushed for that meeting or school. Well, it's the same concept with red flags. Most of us have had negative experiences whether it was dealing with a narcissist or the misfortune of an abusive relationship. Nonetheless, I'm sure there have been times where you looked back and spot the warning signs that you either ignored or failed to realize at that moment. I know from my experience, there were more than enough red flags present.

So, the question is, why do we choose to ignore our gut instincts and continue to engage with something or someone who we know is clearly going to cause heartbreak or trouble in our lives? This could be for a number of reasons. It could be that you haven't mastered setting boundaries, that you lack self-worth, that your eager and yearn for love so much that you settle, or it could be that there's some inherent belief that you're hard to love or not worthy of the love you deserve. No matter what the reason is, the act of reflecting on these experiences help to empower you moving forward in your healing and self-development process. The most important thing here is to recognize where you fall short as well as pinpointing those red flags that you missed or ignored, so that the next person or thing that tries to enter your life, you can properly discern if they are good to have access to you or if access is denied.

I know everyone has their own perspective of what constitutes a red flag, but I'll share what that means to me. Red flags are simply behaviors, or anything for that matter, that creates doubt and are warning signals of potential future danger, destruction or something that is just not in alignment. I love that word. If you're like me, you tend to believe in the inherent goodness of all people and this is usually what gets you in trouble. If you agree that this is also you, stop this today. Ignoring the red flags because you choose to see the good in people will cost you so much later. Trust me. I've never believed the statement "when people show you who they are, believe them" more than I do now.

I also used to move with the mindset that the first time is a mistake, and the second time is a choice. Another big NO. Never give someone or something multiple chances to hurt or disrespect you. If you combine that faulty inherent goodness projection and the chance giver with a lack of self-love, well, this is why we usually end up loving, trusting, and giving ourselves to people or things that never truly deserved us in the first place. Being in a repetitive cycle of this kind of experience has brought me here to this place today.

The place of "I've been there and I've done that", but now I'm at the point where I want to be better, do better and tolerate nothing less than that. When you are really intentional during this reflection period, when you're moving forward, those red flags will be so clear that you won't need to see if it'll happen again. It's a deal-breaker and it's already out the door. *Don't let the door hit you where the good Lord split you!*

Now, how do you identify those deal breakers? Well, first you have to reflect on the red flags of your past experiences. I will share a list of red flags, both that were overlooked and some that were, unfortunately for me, ignored. Ignoring red flags only really happens for the men that I've already developed attachments to or in the process of falling for them. Also, a major factor in the two is that sex was probably involved.

These scenarios consist of a man whose charm and affection completely took over the logic part of my brain and compelled me to ignore my intuition. These red flags range in levels of what the *fuck*, but these are the ones that I have reflected on from my experience. And before you read on, I'd like to make a disclaimer that these are real life scenarios. As much as I'd like to say these are fake, I cannot make these things up.

1. **What the F*CK?!**
   He would frequently ask me about my interest in threesomes. Turned out he practiced polygamy and wanted me to be his second wife. Yes, you read correctly. His *second* wife.

2. **Holy F*ck!**
   He would randomly become angry, irritable, dump ash trays to possibly find marijuana and pretty much couldn't function without it. Turned out he was bipolar.

3. **Oh F*ck!**
   Their (because there were multiple) ex-girlfriends would stalk, message and harass me. From fake Instagrams to Google numbers, I was *really* being stalked and harrassed. But, I allowed the men I was dating to convince me that they were crazy, making things up, or lying. Although I believe they were crazy for doing those things, it turned out (in both scenarios) they both were still dating their ex-girlfriends.

4. **Are You F*cking Serious?**
   There was only admission to lies where they were caught. Full disclosure was never offered on their own accord.

5. **F*ck That!**
   "That's just how I am". This one is my favorite. That is toxicity at its best. It's a cop out for people who lack accountability and too lazy to change their behavior because it requires too much work and self-confrontation.

See, I told you. There are levels. Yes, I know. These are embarrassing. However, I am at a place where I feel comfortable to openly talk about my experiences because I am at a place of emotional freedom, reached a level of forgiveness and detachment from those experiences after being intentional with my reflection and healing process. I no longer label or identify anything as a red flag anymore.

Anything that provokes a doubt within me, it's cut out of my life. It's a deal breaker. This prevents even the slightest probability that someone will lead me down the wrong path who relies on deceit, manipulation and charm (or their representative, as I like to call it), to ease their way into my life. You want to know why? It's all thanks to that alarm clock that protects me. And trust me, it only takes one time for the sound of the alarm to go off. There's no snooze button with the deal breaker.

VI

LISTEN TO YOUR GUT

"When something feels off, it is."

—*Abraham Hicks*

Whether you call it gut instinct or intuition, listen to it. Now before I go on to explain the lesson in this, I must first make an important point for you to learn before the application of this lesson. Do not confuse intuition and instinct with unresolved trauma. You have to be able to distinguish whether it's your intuition guiding you or whether it's your trauma misleading you. So, in the case that you think it may be your trauma that's misleading you, 1) you probably shouldn't be dating right now and 2) ask questions for clarity instead of moving based on the story that you've created in your head that may or may not be true. Clarity indeed preserves relationships.

That being said, have you ever had a time when you felt that something was just off or was not quite right? Have you felt a sense to do something but didn't act on it? Have you ever caught bad vibes about a person and then ignored it? I have and it's okay if you have too. From here on out, pay more attention to what your gut or intuition speaks. When you don't listen to your intuition, you are betraying yourself. When you betray yourself, you in turn set yourself up to be betrayed. Your gut feeling and intuition is a knowing that is much deeper and beyond the logic of your mind. And if you slow down and align yourself with God, that intuition is essentially the way that God speaks and guides you.

Let me be clear. There is human instinct and gut feelings. I believe those to be the things that nudge us in certain directions or alert us to threats or danger. For the most part, those instincts are usually accurate and will guide you on the journey that is highest for your growth, regardless of the actual physical outcome. You will know it's your gut or intuition because you will feel the power of its direction.

It might make you scared or reluctant, but deep down you will feel that it simply feels right. Then, there's what I like to call God's Spirit in the form of my intuition. These are similar and connected, but this type of intuition is different and more powerful because it works above and beyond our physical senses. When you're aligned with God, he attunes you to his answer, his way of doing things. He also evokes this extraordinary peace that enables us to do what he wants, even if we're scared.

John 16:13 says, "When He, the Spirit of truth, has come, He will guide you into all truth ... whatever He hears He will speak; and He will tell you things to come"[5]. This means trusting your intuition is trusting the collection of your experiences as you've walked with the Lord. Your intuition holds all the insights you've gained as you've studied the Bible, prayed, reflected on your experiences, read thoughtful books, listened to sermons, and more. To truly trust your intuition and act on it, is to take responsibility for your reality and experience. When you do this, you own your power.

To really step into the better, new and improved versions of yourself, it requires that you

---

5 John 16:13 NKJV

listen to and act on your intuition. There may be many times in your life when what you are guided to do won't make sense in the moment. However, it's only when you act on your intuition that life will later reveal the "Why?". So, when you feel that instinct or hear that voice, rather than over analyzing "Why?", which often paralyzes you from taking action, simply listen to it and obey it. As you take that step, life will reveal what you need to know as you need to know it. So trust it.

VII

IF YOU FOCUS ON THE PACKAGE, YOU'LL MISS THE GIFT

"Don't judge a book by its cover, you might miss out on a great story."

—*Unknown*

Don't let that go over your head. If you focus on the package, you will miss the gift. Whew. Let's talk about it. I have definitely been guilty of this big mistake. Let me help you visualize this a little bit. You know every holiday season around Christmas time, everyone does a Secret Santa or Elephant Gift Exchange. If you don't know what those are, a Secret Santa is when you're secretly assigned a person to gift a present and an

Elephant Exchange is when a group of people purchase a gift under a certain monetary value and everyone takes turns picking a gift.

We all know the saying, "Don't judge a book by its cover", right? Right. But, when it comes to gifts, we are definitely judging the gift by its size. No one wants the tiny gift because, honestly, what could that be? It obviously can't be of value. Wrong. This is a great analogy for dating and relationships. What this essentially means is that most of us spend so much time focusing on the outer appearances and what we want and in turn bypass what we actually need, the gift.

Back to the analogy, you can pick a small box and there could be a $10 gift card to Starbucks in it or it can be Air pods or a diamond ring. You can also pick the biggest box in the bunch and get lucky with a brand-new juicer or end up with a box full of air and a Crackle Barrel T-shirt. The point of this is to say that looks can be deceiving. Just because it looks good, doesn't mean it's good or good for you. You could meet a great person, male or female, who looks amazing, body of a goddess, perfect smile, great hair, or muscles of steel. However, that person could also be an asshole, dishonest, selfish, lack emotional intelligence, can't hold a substantive conversation and more. They looked good, but you ended up with that nice big box filled with air and a measly t-shirt.

There has definitely been a time in my life, and I'm sure there may have been more, where I possibly missed out on my blessing from focusing on the package. If you asked me a few years ago, "What's your type?" or "What are you looking for from a guy?", I would have started off by naming what I wanted: I wanted a tall (6'0), dark chocolate, fit and muscular, pretty smile and ambitious man. The list didn't stop here but this is what I *started* with and at the moment felt most important to me. In my eyes, as long as those were met, if the rest didn't follow, I'm sure they could be learned. I know. Horrible. But this is what I mean by focusing on the package.

I've stayed in situations that were toxic and detrimental to my health because the package was what I wanted, I just needed them to get the internal part right. I would justify my staying by saying "things take time", "nobody's perfect" or "we have to continue to learn each other". Big no no. Unfortunately, I have also turned down or found excuses to not be with great men. There has been an instance where a man was perfect and had maybe one or two minor issues (ones that weren't self-compromising or harmful) that deterred me from being with them. There has also been a man that was just not my type at all physically but was EVERYTHING I wanted and needed emotionally, spiritually, and mentally.

What I learned is that the things that we usually want are the things we lust. I was lusting for a tall, dark-skinned, fit gym-rat like myself. But that's not what I needed. Not to say that our blessing cannot come in the form that we desire. I'm saying that it shouldn't be the only thing being sought. You shouldn't be so caught up in what you "want" that you ignore other options that could be your person. During my periods of stillness and reflection, I often prayed and made a list of what it was that I was looking for. That list changed and now has three sections: 1) what I need (which is the most important to me), 2) what I want, and 3) things that are extra. If you read my journal today, this is what it reads:

Things that I need:
1) *Integrity*
2) *Believer/Has community*
3) *Honest/Open*
4) *Ambition*
5) *Emotional intelligent*

6) *Family-oriented*
7) *Goal-oriented*
8) *Emotionally available*
9) *Handles conflict positively*
10) *Accountability*
11) *Good heart*
12) *Self-love*
13) *Compassion*
14) *Teacher/Student*
15) *Not judgmental*
16) *Passionate*
17) *Alignment*
18) *Good financial habits*
19) *Communicator*
20) *Working on trauma*
21) *Loves me for me.*
22) *Understanding*
23) *Fit – Prioritizes health*
24) *Identity*

Things that I want:
1) **Tall**

I've experienced so much trauma because of my lack of discernment and my choice in men. That initial list I had, had me chasing after men that looked good but were far from good for me.

And if you noticed, the "things that are extra" list doesn't exist. Why? Because those are things that I no longer entertain, that no longer matter when it comes to who someone is as a person, their heart, and integrity. When you experience cycles of trauma and toxic relationships, you gain baggage and emotional debt. If you never learn and continue this cycle, by the time your person arrives, you won't be able to receive them properly.

Put it like this, we all know what debts are. Most of us have student loan debt, car payments and mortgages. But there's also those unseen debts that we accrue that live within our hearts like emotional debt. Stop accruing emotional debt from people you should have never invested in. Just like the more monetary debt you have, the harder it will be to pay down. The more emotional debt you have, the harder it will be for the one God has for you to help you get out of that debt or coexist with you for that matter. Even worse, the person God has for you may then encounter collateral damage for something they had nothing to do with. Collateral damage is injury inflicted on something other than an intended target. You don't want that and they don't deserve it.

So, the lesson here is don't miss out on a blessing just because it is not packaged the way you expect it should be. Know what you need but make sure that you aren't elevating personal preferences over character. You will save yourself so much trouble and heartache by focusing on what's important. Blessings are like glitter. You don't always see them until you look from a different perspective.

VIII

TRUST HAS TO BE EARNED

"Trust is earned when actions meet words."

—*Chris Butler*

I used to approach dating and relationships with the mindset that this is a new relationship and therefore it should be given a clean slate. You know how the school system works with the grading system, right? Everyone starts at an A and the grade changes from there depending on the caliber of work that you complete. Your grade will either drop, remain at the A, or it could increase to an A+. That was my approach to dating. I would start people off at an A. That means I trusted them until they gave me a reason not to.

A MAJOR do NOT. I'm not saying walk into your next relationship with trust issues *cues Drake*. Trust to a certain extent but don't put anything pass anyone. Regardless of how you feel about someone, know that people are capable of any and everything.

Trust is "relying on the integrity or ability of another person."[6] Your ability to truly trust someone is based on their character, not yours. Trust should be earned, not freely given. Trust is one of the most critical elements of any healthy relationship. Rome wasn't built in a day and neither is a healthy relationship. It takes time to learn how to trust and communicate with each other.

I want to tell you a story that is the staple to the premise of this chapter. This is the story of my previous relationship. To make sure that names are not revealed, I will refer to him as John Doe. So, I met my ex-boyfriend during the orientation of my first year in law school. We connected almost immediately. We spent almost every day together for six months for the first semester. Everything was natural and it felt almost too perfect, too good to be true.

I would often say that to myself, but would always remind myself that I am worthy of what

---

[6] Trust definition courtesy of yourdictionary.com

I want and deserve. At that moment, I felt as though that was what I wanted. We both worked full-time while attending law school at night. Everything just aligned. He was so sweet and he was my first taste of what it felt like to be treated right for once. We would have such deep conversations and we would often tell each other "I prayed for you". Of course, we did the disclosures of our past traumas and experiences. He told me that he would never do those things to me that I experienced. I had zero doubts about him. There were no red flags. So, I trusted John Doe.

At the conclusion of our first semester of law school, we decided to celebrate with a vacation to Mexico. The vacation was such a beautiful experience. We were so happy that we were constantly stopped by resort staff and strangers telling us how "in love" we looked. We even decided to make things official on that trip. I will never forget how I felt during those six months. I know this is supposed to be a story with a lesson and you're probably wondering why I will never forget how I felt during those beautiful six months.

Well, to my surprise, we returned home to something I would have never expected. One night we decided to stay the night at his place (he lived in the basement of his parents' house). It was my first time there and it just felt exciting, you know? Like sneaking out of your parent's house. (By the way, I've never done that.) It was something new. Beautiful night.

The next morning, we are sleep and I hear the door crack open. I hadn't yet met his family, so I assumed it might have been a family member. I pull the blanket closer to my face and attempt to go back to sleep, hoping that whoever that was went away. Nope. This person, who shall be referred to as Angry Amy, comes into the room and stands to the side of the bed where I was laying. I turned around and opened my eyes to Angry Amy standing with her arms crossed. She looked like she had a lot to say.

There was a bit of an awkward silence in the room. John Doe looked uncomfortable, Angry Amy looked, well, very angry, and I was confused. I initially asked John Doe "who is this?", but he was stuck and silent. I then said out loud, "please tell me you're his sister". Angry Amy replied, "Go ahead John Doe, tell her." Nothing was said from John Doe. I reply, "tell me WHAT?!". I look at him, and nothing. Angry Amy is still saying, "Tell her. Tell her who I am." After a few minutes of silence, Angry Amy decides to tell me who she is.

Pain Into Power

She says, "You're supposed to know about me." *Oh gosh, what does that mean.*

She continues and says, "You're supposed to know about me and he's been hiding you from me. We're supposed to be sharing you." *Sharing me?* At this point, I had enough. I looked at him and demanded an answer. He is still quiet and has the dumbest look on his face. Here goes Angry Amy again. She says, "John Doe practices polygamy and I am his girlfriend. John Doe wants two wives and we are actively looking for our third partner. He usually keeps me in the loop but he's been hiding you, going behind my back and lying." I couldn't believe the words that came out of her mouth.

I was shocked. I think both my heart and stomach fell out of my butt after I heard that. I was hurt. Actually, hurt is an understatement. Those beautiful six months went up in flames. That was no longer the reality anymore. Everything that happened between us was a lie. Those six months painfully flashed through my head and cut so deep because I knew I had to walk away. I immediately asked John Doe if I could talk to him alone. Angry Amy storms off and leaves the house. I begin asking 101 questions. "John Doe, what the hell? Are you serious? You lied to me this entire time! Why didn't you tell me upfront?!".

I don't remember the nuts and bolts of the conversation after Angry Amy left, but one thing that will stick with me forever is his response to my question of "why weren't you honest?". He looked me in my eyes and told me in the most serious, "sincere" voice, "I didn't tell you the truth because I knew you didn't want that and I didn't want to lose you. I wanted to make you fall in love with me first so that you'd be more understanding." *Are you kidding me?!* Ladies and gentlemen, if you're reading this, I cannot. make. this. up.

Sometimes I still can't believe that happened to me. I thought I had experience all there was to experience when it came to bogus situations. The joke was all the way on me. However, I tell you this story to say, don't be quick to trust everyone immediately. Don't trust everything you see. Even salt looks like sugar. The worst part about the situation is that he genuinely believed that it was okay. He looked me in my eyes and basically told me that despite knowing this was bad for me, would hurt me, and wouldn't make me happy, he did it anyway because it was what *he* wanted.

Most people are motivated by their own self-interest; therefore, your best interest may be at stake. This was a very deceptive act. I call it evil. Deception is the act of encouraging people to believe information that is not true. John Doe was intentional with his actions. He was so focused on what it was that he wanted that he was willing to put my heart on the line as long as his needs were met. That is a dangerous person. Not only does it show a lack of concern for anyone else, it also shows that you are not a person of your word.

So, moral of the story is, when it comes to trust, you have to be careful not to get ahead of yourself but you also have to be careful not to be stingy on trust either. Look for a balance in the give and take of trust and also the patterns of what your partner does with the trust you give them. This is applicable for all types of relationships, not just romantic ones. With trust comes vulnerability and you must be able to discern whether this person, be a partner, friend or family member, will protect you at all costs. "Consistency earns trust and inconsistencies earn doubt." Pay attention.

IX

STOP TRYING TO FIGURE IT OUT

"Whatever is meant for me will be enough. Whatever misses me cannot fill me up."

—*Rob Hill Sr*

This is a good one. You have to stop trying to make unnecessary meaning of everything. It's natural for us to want to know the reasons behind why things happen in our life. Why did he breakup with me? Why didn't I get the job? Why her and not me? The list goes on. If something doesn't make sense, you feel like you have to make sense of it, otherwise you'll never stop thinking about it. We often spend so much time dwelling on the past and trying to figure out what it means that we fail to be present and move forward. I love the saying, "God put eyes in the front of our head so we can see what is coming, not where we came from." Let it go. I promise eventually it will all make sense.

There are questions to which answers sometimes do not exist. There are also answers that just generate more questions. Sometimes, answers and solutions can only be made from having lived something out, saw it through, and tried. Life isn't clear cut and there will always be gray areas. The biggest thing I learned from my experiences is to stop trying to figure out other people's behavior. I figured, if I can figure out the reason, I can probably fix the problem. So, I engaged in obsessive speculation. Maybe this is why this happen or maybe his daddy issues are the reason for his lack of direction. I don't know. Just trying to put meaning to something.

I never really had a problem with introspection. It's nothing for me to examine the reasons for my own behavior. However, it is a different ball game trying to discover the reasons for someone else's action. Have you heard of outrospection? Yeah, me either. Actually, Microsoft Word has it underlined in red. It isn't a word and it's because you're not supposed to do it. So, from here on out, change your ways. Instead of wondering and speculating the actions of someone else, just take recognition and act accordingly. Why people do the things that they do is none of your business. It is not for you to analyze. That is their job. Your job is to simply pay attention, and to make informed decisions based on what you see.

I know this seems easier said than done. You want to solve the problem that you see. However, you have to learn and understand that the solution does not lie in trying to get other people to change. I'm going to throw that Maya Angelou quote at you one more time. "When people show you who they are, believe them."[7] People can be and do whatever it is that they choose to be or do. That is their business. The only thing that you can control is your own behavior. You can let go of what's not important, put in place firm boundaries around what is important, and use your brain to discern what is working for you and what isn't.

Also, most of the time when we're trying to figure things out, it's always something negative or not to our liking. That can lead to overthinking that will make you uneasy and feeling bad about yourself. Overthinking leads to negative thoughts which aren't true, and sometimes you'll end up

---

7   The one and only Maya Angelou.

believing them. Once you start to believe those thoughts, now you've opened that door allowing and giving them power to destroy your inner peace and happiness. Having the answer to every situation or feeling is not how life works. You figure it out by living. You figure it out by seeking advice and not taking it, by making mistakes and learning from them, and by missing that opportunity that you wanted so bad. Just know that everything always works out in the end. We're not in control anyway.

Move on, but don't move on holding resentment and grudges. It's a waste of energy. Some wrongs that are done to us have purpose, believe it or not. They are for our growth and transformation. Even the butterflies have to digest themselves before transforming into beautiful creatures. Some experiences are necessary and inevitable for our highest good. To bring this to perspective, I'll tell you about the Job story in the Bible because it is a good representation of this.

The Book of Job addresses the questions that many of us have in trying times: why do bad things happen to good people? Where is God in our suffering? The storyline is simple. Job was a wealthy, wise, humble and charitable man. So, one day Satan appears before God and asked if he could test Job's righteousness and fidelity. God gave permission but insisted that Satan not physically harm him. Satan arranged for Job's animals, servants and children to be killed. Upon learning of his tragic loss, Job fell to the ground in grief but did not blame or insult God. He actually still blesses God in his prayers. In other words, he didn't fail the test.

Not satisfied with this outcome, Satan returned to God and requested that he test Job's righteousness even more. Once again, God gave the green light for further testing but again insisted that Job's life be unharmed. So, Satan struck Job with a terrible skin disease. Upon witnessing her husband's suffering, Job's wife encouraged him to blame God, but he remained faithful. Some friends then visited Job and offered consolation. During their consolation, they essentially tried to get Job to give up his piety, but Job remained steadfast in his faith. In the end, God returned and rewarded Job for his fidelity by returning his wealth, providing him with twice as much property and new children.

The moral of the tale is this: when you are faced with hard times, don't be tempted to relinquish your faith in God. God has reasons beyond your understanding for what he is doing, and if you hold on to your faith long enough, God will show you the purpose behind your pain. So, inhale positivity, exhale negativity. It happened. Reflect, apply and press on. Onward and forward. And do it with love.

X

YOU CAN'T CHANGE PEOPLE

"You cannot change the people around you. But you can change the people that you choose to be around."

—*Unknown*

You can't change people, so don't drive yourself crazy trying to. Instead, just change how you deal with them. The main reason why you can't change people is because accountability feels like an attack when you're in denial and not ready to acknowledge your behavior and how it affects others. Someone who isn't committed to growing will not change. Not to say that people can't change, because they can. But people won't change unless they want to. It's not in your hands.

If you remember from the red flags are deal breakers chapter, one of the most common traits I found in the men I was dating was that they all had the mindset of "It's just the way I am. Take it or leave it." That is self-limiting and it's a disservice to any relationship. I don't know how much time I spent trying to convince people that that was a faulty mindset to possess, but I wasted my time. When you say "this is just how I am", you remove from yourself the possibility of doing better and learning more. You essentially are saying that there's no room for growth. None of us are static, except by choice.

Also, you cannot change what you aren't aware of or refuse to acknowledge. It's really a cop out. You might as well say, "I don't have the motivation to change this aspect of myself". Sometimes, people feel like they have achieved a certain level of self-acceptance and know how they are and simply accepts it. This is fine, but this is where you leave. Stop being so understanding. This understanding is making you look over the disrespect. The "it's just how I am" is certainly a sign of immaturity. As adults, we are responsible for identifying our toxic traits, personal dysfunction and learned behavior and our duty is to unlearn and fix them.

You can inspire someone to change and you can educate them towards change. But you cannot make them change. Trying to make someone do something requires manipulation and coercion. You don't want to do that. Nothing should be forced. Besides, you want someone to do things because they want to, because it's natural for them to do so, not because you told them to do it. Have you ever had to beg for an apology or convince someone that you were deserving of one? How did you feel once you received that apology? When that has happened to me in the past, I know that by the time I finally received an apology, I didn't even want it anymore. It's forced and not genuine. Anything that is forced is not going to be sincere.

If changing someone requires you to intervene in their life, don't do it. Although most people do it with good intention, it's just taking responsibility for another person's actions and emotions, and that's not your job. If you take it upon yourself to try to change the people you choose and allow in your life, you are creating a self-fulfilling prophecy of suffering, disappointment and pain. Trying to force someone to become who you want them to be or who you think they should be is wrong and it's disempowering. You are essentially taking away the responsibility and obligation that they have on their own life. Everyone is responsible for his or her own growth.

Taking an even deeper look at this, if you are basing your self-worth on someone else's capacity to change, I promise you will remain in a vicious cycle of emotional dependence. Don't give someone else the power of determining your worth. You are the only person that should ever be allowed to determine your worth. How people treat you is not a reflection of your worth. "Your value doesn't decrease based on someone's inability to see your worth." I know I just said worth like four times but knowing your worth is the answer to a lot of problems.

Most importantly, you also can't change and shouldn't desire to change how people think about you. What you should strive for is peace and being at peace with who you are. When someone says something dishonest or wants to walk out of your life, instead of spending your energy trying to keep them, confronting people to clear things up, or even reaching out to someone else to validate how you felt hearing it, you should just take it for what it is and keep it moving. Keep moving forward with your energy intact. Stop letting other people change the way you see yourself.

It is so easy and comfortable to tell other people what they should and should not be doing. It's easy to point out other people's flaws and what they should be working on. However, it's not about them. It's about you. Focus on you. Being critical of another doesn't help you in the introspection and self-awareness that you need in order to reach your full potential and become the best version of yourself. Just know that if they wanted to, they will.

XI

LOVE YOURSELF MORE

"How you love yourself is how you teach others to love you."

—*Somebody else probably said this but my mother said this to me too.*

For the fifth time. Know. Your. Worth. Everything will change when you begin to truly love yourself. You no longer will send out energy of desperation. You will become such a powerful source from within that you just attract better.

Remember my story of John Doe and Angry Amy? The guy who led by deceit and manipulation for six months to make me want to be his second wife? It almost worked. He wanted me to fall in love with him so that I'd be more understanding. That statement in its own tells you that some men know the power of love and aim to use and abuse. I actually thought about it. I loved him so much that I actually thought of ways that this could work because I didn't want to lose him. I was so stuck on those six monogamous months that I did not want to leave. I was stressing about what my friends and family would think, how we could actually be together, why he didn't just tell me upfront and give me the opportunity to choose. I honestly felt like a prisoner to his love. I felt like I was stuck.

Of course, me not immediately walking away and knowing that I was worth more than that and deserved more than that, it backfired on me SO bad. Remember, this all took place during my first year in law school. It was almost a reason I didn't finish school, a reason that I was going to give up. I loved him more than I loved myself that I was knowingly and willingly putting myself in a HUGE compromising situation that I knew was bad for me and would hurt me. Sometimes we choose temporary happiness over doing what we know we have to do.

And I wasn't stuck. The main reason why people feel stuck in situations is because their love is rooted in something else.

Pain Into Power

Love doesn't make you feel stuck, it should do the opposite. And this is where introspection and reflection are so important. It's also not the easiest thing to do. You know why? Sometimes it's hard facing yourself. Sometimes it's hard owning up to those ugly things about ourselves because we all love to think highly of ourselves and our image in the highest and brightest light. I remember after each of my failed relationships or dating situations (situationships, as people call them), I would tell my mom everything that happened. I mean *everything*. If you're one of those men that chose to read this, yes, my mother knows and she doesn't like you. *Cues Justin Bieber's "my mama don't like you and she likes everyone"*

Anyways, she would ALWAYS say to me, "Briya, I just don't get it. Do you love yourself? Do you have low self-esteem?". I would get so offended because of course I love myself and no I don't have low self-esteem. *Are you kidding?* I knew I was attractive, had it going on, was smart and the whole package. That's just surface level, but I really believed that on top of that, I really loved myself. WRONG. It took me a looooooooong time to acknowledge that I didn't really love myself and I hadn't been properly loving myself for all of my dating life.

It took some deep digging, and I mean deep, to realize that. When people hear the words such as insecure and codependent, no one wants to attribute that to themselves. It's negative. That was me.

As beautiful as that butterfly giving, make my foot pop when we kiss, intense love may seem to be, there is a fine line between that and co-dependency. When I said before that I felt stuck, I wasn't stuck. I was co-dependent. When you're codependent, the love you have is rooted so deeply in feelings of low self-esteem, insecurity, inadequacy, fear of being rejected, and the most important, just wanting to be loved. You must never get to the point of wanting love so bad that you settle for the first thing that looks close to it. Co-dependency results in you losing yourself and who you are in a sense and focusing completely on the needs of the other person.

I remember doing things that I was uncomfortable doing, to make John Doe happy. I remember crying so much from being hurt that he deceived me, but still thinking of how I could make him happy because I didn't want to hurt him. I remember not wanting to leave (or for him to leave Angry Amy) because I felt like I would never find anyone like him again. Honestly, typing this makes me cringe. But, sometimes the only way to learn is by getting it wrong. When I reflected on this, I asked myself what am I lacking that I felt the need to compromise myself like that? Why did I love him so much? Did I really love him? Why do I want love so bad that I'm blatantly and carelessly ignoring things that are destructive to my peace of mind, my emotional well-being and my heart? READ THAT LAST SENTENCE AGAIN.

Co-dependency is so destructive. It's destructive in the sense that someone who is codependent, lacks the necessary qualities of self-esteem, self-worth and assurance that accompany healthy relationships. A codependent person will make excuses for someone else's toxic habits. It will also have you staying in a situation where you don't belong for all of the wrong reasons. You should reach a level contentment and value of yourself that it doesn't matter who stays or who goes. You maneuver in a way that your actions scream I'm good with or without you because I love myself.

All relationships require some form of give and take, but you should never and will never have to compromise your morals for something that is meant for you. And I promise you, you won't get anything that you prayed for until you become the type of person that should receive it.

XII

DON'T SETTLE

Don't settle for less just because it's available.

When you don't love yourself and lack self-esteem, you always end up settling for less than what you deserve. Settling means letting go things that are important to who you are, what you believe in, and how you would like to be treated and loved. We settle when we start compromising ourselves and our own needs. Sometimes we stay in relationships out of fear of being alone. Remember, if you don't love yourself, you will always be chasing after people who don't love you either.

Let me tell you of the story that brought me to this awakening and to writing this book. On September 27, 2020, I was attacked by a woman whose name moving forward will be Bunny. She almost killed me that night and unfortunately, it was for nothing. I had been dating this guy, we'll name him Jamal, for a few years but without a title. When we initially met, he made his disclosure that he wasn't ready for a relationship because he didn't have time, he was working on his goals, and he was still dealing with traumas from his previous relationship. At the time, I wasn't ready for a relationship either, so, I decided I still wanted to date and get to know him.

So, for about three years him and I had intimate relations and continued to get to know one another with no strings attached. Well, at least on his end. Eventually, I started to catch feelings and wanted more despite his constant disclosure of still not being ready and STILL dealing with past trauma. Because he explicitly didn't state that he didn't want to be with me and because he would tell me how great of a woman I was, I fell for potential. I was focused on what could be and the possibility of him changing his mind that I failed to accept what was. I was settling. There were things that I knew he was doing that I didn't necessarily liked or agreed with—such as keeping his options open, dating other people, being intimate with other people, and more—but I still stayed around because I thought I couldn't express what I wanted or that it would matter.

Fast forward to September 27, 2020, I was invited to his place for his best friend's birthday party. The night went well until about 2A.M. as I was headed to my car to go home. Jamal came to my car to talk about something and we sat in the car for a while. Then, Bunny approaches my vehicle at the passenger door, bangs on the window, requesting that Jamal gets out. Jamal stated that he'd be there in a minute. Jamal and I continued to talk. I'm not sure how much time passed by but Bunny came back a second time and she was angry. She returns to the passenger window, bangs on it much harder this time and says, "You're treating this bitch like she's your girlfriend. Get out of the car, I'm going to punch you in the face."

Jamal gets out of the car and Bunny becomes irate and is yelling and hitting him. So, I get out of the car to help deescalate the situation. That did not go well. I got out of the car, approached the back of my vehicle and stated, "It's okay, we were just talking...", and before I could finish my sentence, she was charging at me and yelling and next thing you know she was hitting me. There were few people around but no one could get her off of me.

There was one moment where I sitting on my butt on the ground and Bunny had my head in her arms and was suffocating me. I remember panicking because I was losing air and I thought I was going to die. I remember saying, "Jamal, get her off of me, I can't breathe." The vessels in my right eye had burst due to the suffocation. My face was injured really badly, my contacts were knocked out, my shoes and clothes went missing in the process, I could barely walk, and I was on bedrest for a week.

It turned out that Jamal had been dating her as well and invited multiple women to his house that night that he'd been dating. I was so embarrassed. I was hurt. To make matters even worse, I decided to pursue charges and when the cops arrived, Jamal didn't want to help. He said, "I care about you both and don't want anything to happen to either of you." He was reluctant to help, even though he was the main witness, he barely checked on me, and the fact that I was seriously injured and almost died because of him (partly) and that didn't affect him, really broke me. I couldn't believe someone that I was giving myself to for years didn't care enough about me to simply just tell the truth.

However, not only were there red flags, there were things that Jamal would say and do prior to that incident that I knew was not okay or to my liking that I chose to keep a blind eye to. I chose to see the good in him and made excuses because I was holding onto potential. I settled. Remember when I said choosing to focus on the good in people will cost you later? This one costed me BIG time. I almost lost my life. All of this is why you should never settle. When you settle for less than what you deserve, you get less than what you settled for. And sometimes it takes losing what you were settling for to remember what you deserve.

I know failed relationships can be emotionally and mentally taxing and can create doubt that you'll ever be loved correctly. Remember, you are worthy of the love that you desire. You just have to believe it. Stand firm in who you are, what you want, and your convictions. No more betrayal of your intuition. Step into your power by stepping into your truth. Don't deny, avoid or suppress any part of what makes you, you. Always stay true to who you are. That means always upholding what is it that you want. Remember that you will not get what you want until you become the type of person that should receive it.

XIII

INVEST IN YOURSELF

Don't be upset by the result you didn't get with the work you didn't do.

The final and most important lesson that I've extracted from my experiences is the importance of investing in yourself. The time, effort, and sometimes money that you invest in yourself will have a direct impact on the quality of life that you experience now and in the future. When I say invest in yourself, I'm talking about self-care, tender, love and caring. Self-care is the deliberate action of taking care of your emotional, spiritual, mental, and physical health. As simple as this concept seems to be, it is often the most overlooked. Many people tend to neglect their own self-care because they are focused on others or other things more than themselves. We're investing in our education, our career, friendships, homes, and children, but rarely our own personal wellness or heart's desire.

When you become too focused and consumed with other people or things, you can lose yourself. That's why it is important to have some serious "me time." Self-care is doing the things that physically make us feel good, like bubble baths and massages, but it's also the internal work too. That includes attending therapy sessions, reading self-help books, bible studies with friends, meditating and whatever that looks like for you. It's a place of transformation and choosing to believe that you deserve to and can change your life.

A major part of the internal work is sitting with yourself. This is a journey, one that may not be easy, but certainly worth it. Whatever it is that is holding you back or weighing you down, you have to find time to grieve and then let go of the heaviness. This is a journey on how to love yourself and really understand what we need to fill ourselves up. After all, the most important relationship of all is the one you have with yourself. And, the relationship you have with yourself sets the tone for every other relationship you have. Just know that you won't wake up one day to a magically different life like a romanticized Disney Channel movie. This takes intentionality and real work.

Throughout your life, can you guess the person who you're guaranteed to always be with? You guessed right, it's yourself. If you don't know what makes you happy outside of other people, you'll always feel like your emotional well-being is at the mercy of external factors. But, if you take advantage of that "me time", you'll become more in-tune with your emotions and get clear on what it is you want most in life, regardless of outside influences. You become a better version of yourself. That's always the goal.

It's usually the smallest changes that you make that end up creating the biggest differences. Your daily choices and habits will transform your life into something that you will enjoy living. You have to train your mind to be stronger than your doubts, your emotions, and sometimes your thoughts. Creating change is certainly much harder than desiring it. This is much similar to it being easy to get motivated, but being discipline is the challenge. Why? Because often times the judgment and expectations we have for ourselves get in the way of our goals and things we should be doing. However, you must remember that if you are not changing, you are choosing. Change doesn't happen by chance, it happens by choice. To live the life we've never had before, we must become someone we've never been.

So, say yes to you. Find an inner happiness and peace that doesn't depend on anyone else. Your well-being and happiness matter just as much as anyone else's. You deserve space to cultivate growth and healing. You deserve time to rest and reset. Remember, you cannot pour from an empty cup. Caring and investing in yourself is not self-indulgence, it's self-preservation.[8]

---

[8] You already know. Audrey Lorde said it first.

PART III

GROWTH

XIV

GOD

God is the best listener. You don't need to shout, nor cry out loud. Because he hears even the very silent prayer of a sincere heart.

I want to first start off by saying this journey of growth, self-development and maturation is all because of the relationship I've cultivated with God during my times of stillness and finding community. It has really changed my life from how I see things, how I handle things and drive why I do the things that I do. However, let me say that I was not always like this. I was not intentional in the past. I wanted to build a relationship with God, but I always made excuses about time and not knowing where to start. Therefore, I never got around to it.

I will tell you this. Sometimes God will let you hit rock bottom so that you will discover that He is the rock at the bottom. *Whew*. I know. I'll say it again. God will *let* you fall down so that you will discover that he is the ground beneath you. There are things that happen in our lives that happen to bring us closer to God. For me, that was all of my failed relationships, loss and pain. With each one, I felt like there were voices bringing me closer and closer to God. However, it was me almost losing my life on September 27th that made me realize that I needed God.

During hard times, those periods of the crushing, the pressing, or the molding, you have to face it. If you avoid this process, you avoid your calling. We cannot become what God is calling us to be if we are avoiding the molding process. When God is calling you to do or be something, there is a part of you that needs to die or be set to the side or else it will hinder you and limits what He can do for you. Devastation matures you as a believer. This is the time where God does deep work on you. Character is being built. I'm a walking testimony to that. It really gives me chills. My greatest loss created one of my greatest victories. This book. Life will test you just before it will bless you.

In order to get to this point, you have to believe and you have to have faith. "Faith is the assurance of things hoped for, the conviction of things not seen."[9] A good biblical story that I like to reference is the parable in Matthew 13:3-9. This is the Parable of the Sower or the Parable of the Four Soils. The four soils are the hard ground, the stony ground, the thorny ground and the good ground.

The Parable of the Sower concerns a sower who scatters seeds, which falls on four different types of ground. The hard ground "by the way side" prevents the seed from sprouting at all, and the seed becomes nothing more than bird food. The stony ground provides enough soil for the seeds to germinate and begin to grow, but they don't take root and wither in the sun. The thorny ground allows the seed to grow, but the competing thorns choke the life out of the beneficial plants. Finally, the good ground receives the seed and produces much fruit.

The seed was the same in every place, but the condition of the soil was different. The soil represents our hearts and the seed represents the word of God. In order to get to this place of contentment, growth and understanding, you have

---

9 Hebrews 11:1 NKJV

to be the good ground. If your foundation isn't sturdy, you'll break. Your faith and belief have to be so strong that no matter what your circumstances are, you know that everything will be okay. I've learned to remain calm in every situation because I know that God wouldn't put me in something that I couldn't work through. I walk by faith, not by sight.

Finally, understand that God will not cosign anything that's not in his will for you. He has numbered your days and will fulfill every purpose He has for you. Nothing can happen without God's permission and God will not allow a trial unless He has a divine purpose for it. If you keep your peace, God will always bring you out much better than you were before. Isaiah 43:2 says "when you pass through the waters, I will be with you; and through the rivers, they shall not overflow you. When you walk through the fire, you shall not be burned, nor shall the flame scorch you."[10]

It doesn't matter who's for you, all that matters is who's *with* you. God will always be there with you, no matter what. Through my time with God, I truly learned that there are gifts in pain. There have been gifts in my pain, my trauma, my loss and my failures. If you don't take anything

---

[10] Isaiah 43:2 NKJV

away from this chapter, take this. The gift of devastation is dependence, the gift of trauma is trust, and the gift of pain is perspective.[11]

And with that, I will end with a prayer to open you up so that you can receive the following messages to come:

Dear Heavenly Father,

Please help us work on our attitude. Teach us how to be more loving, compassionate, patient, obedient, and humble. Strip away the anger, the bitterness, our stubborn ways, laziness, our pride and complacency. Help us become more like you and help us to practice what we preach. Lord, I pray for the renewal of our mind, heart and soul. Especially during these trying times, I ask that you be our peace in the times we can't seem to find it.

I pray for peace over the things that trouble us and the ability to forgive others as you forgive us daily. I pray for stillness in the times we feel the need to fight our own battles. I pray that you give us the discipline to be at peace and let you handle the rest. I pray that you help us forgive ourselves. Lead us not into temptation, but deliver us from

---

[11] Notes from a sermon by Brie Davis, "I'm Glad I Lost"

evil. God, I pray for forgiveness when we've been weak in the flesh. I pray that you open the heart of whoever is reading this to receive you and show us how you respond in the face of failure.

Lord, we thank you for all that you do and continue to do. May we rest our souls in you and trust in your unfailing promises...

In Jesus name we pray, Amen.

XV

FORGIVE YOURSELF

"We can never obtain peace in the outer world until we make peace with ourselves."

—Dalai Lama

The most important lesson during the growth and self-development period is forgiving yourself. It is absolutely imperative that you do this. Being able to forgive yourself requires empathy, kindness, compassion and understanding. You are not perfect. Show yourself some grace. You are still learning. We are all learning. No one in this life has it all together and figured out. Show yourself patience. You're on a journey. This is a marathon, not a sprint.

If we want to make things right, we have to let go. If we continue holding on to the past misdeeds of ourselves, or of others, we will dent our self-esteem and scar the best image of who we can be. Forgiving yourself gives you peace. You stop being a captive to any resentment or grudges you may have and start focusing on other things that are important.

You have to be aware of your limitations and who you are to truly forgive yourself. However, it is important to know that there is no one who has not been hurt or who has not made a mistake. Forgiving yourself makes you realize the position you are as an imperfect being that makes mistakes every now and then. Rather than beat yourself up over every little mistake that you make, you can learn to reap the benefits of forgiveness and be happy.

Withholding forgiveness from yourself and choosing to suffer in self-recrimination doesn't serve anyone and is a disservice to yourself. It may never restore what was lost or undo damage that was done. But, all it does is deprive you of the ability to learn the valuable lessons from your mistakes and prevent you from using your newly gained wisdom to be a greater gift for others. After all, every minute you spend sulking in guilt for what you did wrong is a minute you are not improving yourself and becoming a better you.

Someone once told me that forgiveness was never using the past against someone. Likewise, self-forgiveness is about never again using your fallen moments against yourself. Rather, it is committing to doing your own internal work, confronting oneself with brutal self-honesty and acknowledging the forces that led you to make those mistakes in the first place. And then, the next step is cleaning up your own mess as best you can and recommitting yourself to do better next time. And when you mess up again, as you will because you are human, repeat the cycle.

You are not the mistake. It's important to know that you are *not the mistake*. The action that you took was the mistake. You are separate from it, which means you have the power to choose a different action next time. Jeremiah 31:34 says, "No more shall every man teach his neighbor, and every man his brother, saying, 'Know the LORD,' for they all shall know Me, from the least of them to the greatest of them, says the LORD. For I will forgive their iniquity, and their sin I will remember no more."[12] This does not mean that our all-knowing Father God forgets, but rather, because He forgives us, He chooses not to bring up our sin in a negative way. If God has moved on, shouldn't we do the same?

---

12 Jeremiah 31:34 NKJV

Forgive yourself for not knowing better at the time. Forgive yourself for giving away your power. Forgive yourself for your past behaviors and unhealthy habits. Forgive yourself for the patterns and traits that you inherited while enduring trauma. Forgive yourself for indulging in things that took up and wasted your time but didn't fulfill you. Forgive yourself for declaring yourself as someone you are not. Forgive yourself for all of the times when you didn't add value to others. Forgive yourself for the things that you discovered about yourself that you don't like. Forgive yourself for not correcting what you think you should have. Forgive yourself. Every day is another chance to start over.

XVI

HEAL

"If you don't heal what you hurt you, you'll bleed on people who didn't cut you"

— *Anonymous.*

Here comes another analogy. If an athlete is injured during training or competition, he will need time to recuperate in order to regain his form, strength and power and resume activity. Depending on the severity of the injury, they're off to the hospital with no hesitation and the recovery process may involve some kind of procedure or treatment, applying an ice pack to the injured area, cleaning and stitching it, or simply resting. No matter what the severity is, they're usually told to rest and take it easy.

If someone experiences a blow to the psyche—that is, the mind, soul and spirit—this one is always met with much reluctance to seek help. But as mentioned above, the same should apply for internal healing. Unfortunately, that's never really the case. Vulnerability and human fragility generate fear.

Many of us walk around appearing to be fine on the outside, but in reality, are still hurting on the inside from past traumas, old relationships, familial deaths, or situations that have been left unresolved. There is bitterness, anger and hate that has been festering beneath the surfaces of or mind, hearts and soul. God sees and knows everything and He wants to heal us completely—mind, body and soul. In the recovery process, we can surrender our hurts to Him. As hard as it will be, this is something that we must do. We need to humble ourselves and ask God to heal our hurts so that we can wholeheartedly forgive those who've wronged us. Once we apply the right ointments and astringents to the area, the wound heals on the inside and dries up on the outside.

Now, what you don't want to do is aggravate the injury. The goal is to treat the internal wound. In the sports analogy, aggravating the wound looks like continuing to play basketball on a sprained ankle or knee. In my case, aggravating the injury came in the form of what I like to call serial dating. A serial dater is someone who dates many people without a break in between. Don't get me wrong, I was not out here being intimate with everyone and just dating as a hobby. I just never intentionally dedicated time in between to myself to heal from previous pains. I never truly sat and reflected on why things went the way that they did. I would be open to "getting to know people" and "have friends" but never drew the line to say, "hey, I appreciate the interest, I like you too, but I'm dedicating some time to myself to focus on me and my healing." I just went with the flow and that flow always drifted me into either a relationship or a situationship.

That always backfired on me. I found myself in a cycle learning the same lessons over and over again due to the lack of break, reflection and healing. Even when I did feel those pains, I just closed in, closed down, stayed quiet. I often times even tried to appear the opposite of how I truly felt—strong. Perhaps, it was best to just get through it somehow; not sure how, but somehow. It seemed better and easier to not talk about how I felt. And that's what most of us do.

But, that is not what we deserve. We deserve more than that. If one part of us is hurt, the whole is affected. True respect for ourselves grows out of an acknowledgement of our wholeness. Only then are we able to recognize that in order to care for ourselves, we have to care for all of us.

A life-changing adversity can be crushing. If you let it, the weight of it can keep you flat for a long time. Just know that God will apply the warmth of His love to our hearts, providing peace so that our internal hurts can completely heal. Healing looks different for many people. I would say that although I'm not completely healed from everything that I've experienced, my healing has occurred through the following means:

1. **Bible study and community**
   Find a group of people or a few individuals to grow in God with and study the word. This was the most transformative for me. I started a bible study with two friends that grew in to a huge bible study community that gathered every Tuesday night to discuss and teach each other the word of God.

2. **Prayer**
   I was and am always talking to God, when I'm both happy and sad. It is important to not only

call on Him during times of need and pain. We tend to forget and neglect Him when life is good.

3. **Meditation**
Stretching and sound healing are my main forms of mediation.

4. **Journaling**
I have a personal journal and a devotional journal. The devotional journal is a 52-week scripture, devotional, and guided prayer journal.

5. **Alone time**
Whether it was watching a movie with wine, taking a bath or going to the movies alone, I became comfortable with being alone. Enjoy your own company. Get back to you. Love on yourself. You know your love languages? Well, this is the time to love yourself with those languages.

6. **Abstinence**
I'll say it again. Just stop having sex. It truly brings clarity and a clear mind.

7. **Therapy**

    Invest in a therapist. It's always good to have someone to talk to who isn't biased. Therapists can be so transformative in your healing process.

8. **Reading**

    Reading has always been a passion of mine. Reading will take you places that experience cannot. And with the right book, it'll have you taking notes and changing your thoughts, habits and behavior for the good. Some books that I've read during my healing process are: "The Road Back To You", "You're A Badass", "Master Your Emotions", "The Wait", "Why Men Love Bitches", and "The Way of The Superior Man".

XVII

MASTER YOUR EMOTIONS

"You must be the master of your emotions if you wish to live in peace, for he who can control himself, becomes free."

—Sean Brown

Learn how to master your emotions. When you hear me say "misery into mastery", this is what I mean. This is one that will be an ongoing battle and mastery of training your mind. Sometimes it feels like you can't control what feelings hit you, right? It's so easy to get worked up and overwhelmed when something happens that's not in your interest. But you must cultivate your emotions carefully. What does that mean? I'll tell you.

When you experience emotions, you need to sit with it and dissect it. You need to pinpoint the emotions that are beneficial to your life and let those grow abundantly. The other ones, the ones that sabotage you, you need to weed those out. Don't feed those negative emotions by dwelling on them. And don't accept them and identify with your emotions. You're not a sad person. You are experiencing a sad emotion. You are not your feelings.

One thing that I always preached in my relationships of all types, was that everyone's feelings are valid. You cannot tell someone how they should feel or how they should cope with something. While that is true, it is also important to remember that whatever and however it is that you are feeling, you are responsible for your feelings. I like to remind myself that although my feelings are always valid in the sense that I am my own person, *but*, and that's a big ol' BUT, sometimes those feelings can be irrational. And only you have the responsibility of acknowledging that or you'll always feel attacked. For example, I'll use the recently lost friendship that I discussed in the beginning of the book as an example.

I played matchmaker with my best male friend and, at the time, a really great female friend. I had been best friends with my male friend for over 13 years and had been friends with my female friend for about six months. They began to date for about two months but it ended quickly. After they decided to end their relationship, I continued my friendship with my male friend as I had before they met. My male friend and I had hung out without her knowledge after they ended and she found out through Instagram and blocked me with no explanation or desire to reconcile.

Although her feelings were valid, they were irrational. While I understand being hurt about a failed relationship, it was—in my opinion—irrational to end a friendship of value. If you take a step back from your emotions and communicate or even think to a person's intent, that could avoid a lot of those reactive responses we tend to have in moments like these. The lesson I applied to this situation was boundaries. I don't waste my time trying to explain who I am to people who are committed to misunderstanding me.

Now, let me tell you about my previous emotional control, or the lack thereof. I would let my emotions get the best of me. And I mean the best of me, all of me, take over me. Sometimes, I didn't even know who I turned into. I remember times of anger of being hurt and getting to the point where I was destroying my home. Just letting my belongings have it.

I also remember being so hurt and getting to the point of sulking so much that I felt paralyzed, like I couldn't move on and feeling like I didn't want to be here anymore. You want to know why this happened to me? Because I gave into those feelings in the moment. I fed them. When you do that, your values erode and you will be disconnected from the person that you aspire to be.

When you become aware of your emotions and the feelings they evoke, you can be intentional on the management of your thoughts and behaviors so that no matter what is going on around you, you can maintain your balance, clarity of thought, and sense of inner peace. Our emotions dictate our thoughts, intentions, and actions. When we are aware of our emotions and are able to manage them, we think so much clearer, we make better decisions, and we effectively manage stress and life's inevitable challenges.

On the other hand, if we allow ourselves to live at their mercy, we always end up experiencing some pretty intense situations. And I mean *intense*. Learning to understand your emotions really requires getting serious about developing self-awareness. The major key that I've learned when mastering the misery is understanding the difference between emotions and feelings.

Emotions and feelings are often used interchangeably but there is a difference. Emotions precede feelings and feelings are the next thing that happens after experiencing an emotion. In order to achieve emotional mastery, you have to be able to identify what you're feeling. This is the most powerful thing you can do to create the authentic and fulfilling life we all want and deserve.

So, to take it home, control your emotions, or be consumed and controlled by them. No more being emotionally reactive. You have to train your mind to be stronger than your emotions or else you'll lose yourself every time.

XVIII

BOUNDARIES

"It is necessary, and even vital, to set standards for your life and the people you allow in it."

—*Mandy Hale*

If you're anything like me, this is another good one for you. If you characterize yourself as a people pleaser and often are doing things that you don't want, constantly feeling like people just always cross the line with you, then you have to learn how to set boundaries. What are boundaries? Boundaries define who you are in a relationship. They define what is you and what is not you. The boundaries created in a relationship are meant to set the basic guidelines of how you want to be treated and to establish how others are able to behave around them.[13]

Setting boundaries ensures that relationships are mutually respectful. Boundaries are a form of empowerment. They're a form of strength and a way for us to align with our identity, our desires, and where we stand in the world and in people's life. When you don't have boundaries, you are sending out a signal that you don't know what you want, that you'll take whatever you can get, and that you won't put up a fight along the way. Setting boundaries is a form of self-respect and self-love. By respecting yourself enough to set the necessary boundaries in your life, you'll discover a unique sense of freedom and peace of mind.

Here are some examples of healthy boundaries that I employ while dating, in relationships (familial, romantic and platonic), the workplace or just with myself:

1. Avoiding people who are hurtful, stressful or negative.
2. Not answering work emails, calls and texts on the weekends and after work hours.

---

13 Tracy Hutchinson, PH.D., Psychotherapy and Consulting.

3. Saying no
4. Responsibility and accountability for your own feelings.
5. Asking for space
6. Expressing discomfort
7. Sticking to a budget
8. How you will fight or settle disagreements – does one need space and time to calm down?
9. Tolerances
10. When to engage in intimacy

No matter what your boundaries are, stand firm in them. Boundaries are the limitations that promote healthy relationships, integrity and can preserve relationships. Boundaries can be emotional, physical, spiritual and personal. Remember, boundaries are meant to protect you. Think of them like a fence. A fence is meant to protect your home or designated space. But those fences experience wear and tear from people climbing them and much more. Just like fences, our boundaries will require maintenance. Some people will climb and crawl on our boundaries and test the waters. Most people will respect them if you indicate what they are. But, there will be some people that will require you to constantly remind them of your boundaries and defend them.

Don't feel guilty about setting boundaries either. It's time to stop the self-sabotage, the over-committing and the codependency. We are no longer letting these things permeate our boundaries. This will require daily attention and vigilance, but you got this. Get your hands dirty and do the work of setting and keeping healthy boundaries. Learning to sense and articulate your own needs and choosing where and when to share them should be one of the biggest life changes you should commit to.

XIX

RELATIONSHIPS

"Blessed be the Lord, who has not left you this day...And may he be to you a restorer of thy life, and a nourisher..."

—*Ruth 4:14-15, NKJV*

Because I mentioned that relationships and love have been the *only* aspect of my life that has been troublesome, has caused me to self-destruct and lose myself, it's only right to end with the topic of relationships. After reflecting on all of those lessons, focusing on mastering the misery by practicing and applying these important principles for growth, I now operate differently and approach relationships with more maturity and wisdom.

Briya Brown

Ever since I started my journey of intentionally cultivating my relationship with God and studying His word, the Book of Ruth has definitely been one that I revisit and talk about a lot. The Book of Ruth gives you everything concerning relationships. The story of Ruth and Boaz teaches us about God's timing, value of ourselves and the beauty of wisdom. So, here's how the story went.

Ruth and Oprah, daughters-in-law to Naomi, lost their husbands to death in a foreign land. Naomi, whose husband died ten years prior, decided to return to her homeland. She instructed Ruth and Oprah to leave her since she had no more sons, land or security to offer them. They no longer had an obligation to Naomi and were free to do as the pleased. Ruth and Oprah were from the same place and worshiped the same God, however, their level of faith differed. They had the option of starting a new life with Naomi or staying in Moab. Oprah remains in Moab out of fear. She only had faith in things that she could see. Ruth, on the other hand, suffered from the same loss and decided to lean on what we should always rely on, God. Ruth decided to go with Naomi to Bethlehem.

When Naomi and Ruth returned to Bethlehem, they had to come up with a plan. However,

Naomi was very bitter. Naomi says, "Don't call me Naomi, call me Mara, for the Almighty has dealt very bitterly with me." Can you relate? I can. In the past, during my times of lost, I was always bitter and questioning God and myself and my faith.

Back to the story, so, Ruth decides to be strong for the team and makes a request to Naomi. She asks to go to the field to gather grains and other produce. Just like Naomi and myself, Ruth could've been bitter and upset by her circumstances. She had a husband, a home and a family and now nothing. Nope. Ruth pushed past her pain. They didn't get this far just to get this far. And as we know, God doesn't give us anything he knows we can't handle.

Ruth stayed on the path God led her on and by taking control of her life and using that pain as fuel, she *declared* that she will find that field, there will be grain, it will be enough and that she will find favor. Not only did she declare, she believed. One thing you must take from this is that you must believe that you are going to get what you ask for. So, Ruth goes to the field and stumbles upon Boaz. *Yeah right*. Ruth didn't stumble upon him, it was in God's plan. When Ruth focused on her purpose, in this case, to survive, find work and provide for her family, God was able to move.

When you seek God's direction, commit to your goal and trust Him, he will provide for you.

Now let's get into Boaz. Boaz was a wealthy, knowledgeable and God-fearing man who had a genuine love for family. When Ruth arrived to the field, there were other women working but she stood out because of her determination and focus. However, the most important thing here is that he came in the picture after Ruth started working, not before. Remember that.

Boaz is the husband we all want and need, he possesses the qualities we should look for in our person. But remember the chapter about focusing on the package and you'll miss the gift? Well, these qualities are not ones you'll know by just his look. It's under the surface. Your Boaz may not look like what we think he should and want him to be.

Pastor Jentezen Franklin said it perfectly in his sermon "Boaz Family Tree". I highly recommend after reading this book that you watch it. Pastor Franklin said that Boaz has some relatives and if you don't watch it, you won't get the one that God has for you, you'll get his relatives. Ruth patiently waited for her Boaz. While you're in your singleness, it is imperative that you don't settle for his relatives: Broke-az, Po-az, Lying-az, Cheating-az,

Pain Into Power

Dumb-az, Drunk-az, Cheap-az, Locked up-az, Goodfornothing-az, Lazy-az, and especially his third cousin, Beatinyo-az. Wait on your Boaz and make sure that he respects Yo-az.[14]

If that didn't hit a soft spot, then read it again. Let me tell you. I've had ALL of the relatives and some more. If you are like me, going through vicious cycles and can't for the life of you figure out what went wrong, how you got so caught up, and why you just can't get it right, it's because you have to wait. Stop settling. Stop rushing the process because you are not whole. When you do this, you are attracting someone who is also not whole. You don't attract what you want, you attract who you are. So, take responsibility of what is constantly showing up and you're allowing in your space and life. You may not want to hear it, but it's a direct reflection of what you believe yourself to be and what you believe to be possible.

No matter if you're a glass half full or a glass that's half empty, no matter what you do, you can't fill another without completely emptying your cup. That's not how a relationship is supposed to be and far from what love looks like. You have to be whole and so full. In order to achieve this state

---

14 Jentezen Franklin sermon titled, "Boaz Family Tree".

of being, you have to take that time for yourself. You have to be so comfortable being alone and with yourself and with God. Get comfortable being uncomfortable.

That's how you become full and whole. In turn, what happens then is you attract another whole person. Now guess what will happen when you try to pour into one another while being whole? The cups are running over.[15] There's alignment in vision, goals, beliefs. There's commitment, trust, hope, and communication. All of those things I said in the beginning. There's a solid foundation.

So, moving forward, there's four things that I want you do and always remember. First, attract what it is that you expect. Second, reflect on the things that your heart desires. Third, I need you to become whatever and whoever it is that you respect. And finally, mirror what is it that you admire. Oh, and remember, when you serve according to God's will, your Boaz will find you. Patience is a virtue. It'll definitely be worth the wait.

---

15 This cup analogy was a lesson I learned from one of Rob Hill, Sr.'s books. It's a gem and you should remind yourself of it every time.

PART IV

~

BRIYA 2.0

"Myles Monroe says that the world needs something that God put inside of you. Your gift and your voice!!! And only you have it. And you owe the world that voice and so sometimes if we're not using that voice, the world will knock us down until we find what we're truly here for. What happened to you will bring out the better version of you. EMBRACE IT. The Briya 2.0 needed that story to reach the millions of people she will touch. You are a queen and as royalty you don't run from a challenge, you embrace and overcome it."

—Greg Brown

XX

A LEGACY OF LOVE

"Do everything in love"

—*1 Corinthians 16:14 NKJV*

The message you just read was an Instagram direct message sent to me from a dear friend after I had openly disclosed what happened to me on September 27, 2020. Do you see how God works? Here I am now, five months later with a book telling my story. And God willing, it will reach millions of people and inspire them to explore the darkness and turn their pain into power.

Someone asked me today, "What is the burning question that you're looking to be answered in the current season that you're in?" For me, I am in my awakening season. My answer was, "I feel like the question I had has been answered. My question(s) would be: why? What are you trying to teach me? What are you trying to give me? What is the purpose of all of this pain? What is really my purpose? But I now know that there was a master plan all along. There was purpose behind every trial and tribulation.

God wanted to give me gifts, six gifts to be exact. The first, during my devastation, He gifted dependence. I learned that I need Him and He is the only one I should rely on. He's always in control. The second, through my frustrations, He gifted fruit. For me, it's the fruits of the Spirit: love, joy, peace, kindness, patience, goodness, gentleness and self-control. The third, through my trauma, He gifted trust. Some of my most humbling, difficult experiences have caused a refining of my faith and made me a woman that can now persevere through all storms because I trust in God. I declare and I believe.

The fourth, during my pain, He gave me perspective. The reflection and self-confrontation that I committed myself to has changed how I see things. The fifth, during my loss, He gifted me life. I almost lost my life five months ago. That loss has given me a new life in Christ. I'll never be the same. Finally, the sixth gift, during my grief,

He gave me glory. There is an ugly side of grief, but I've seen through the grace of God how this grief has been used for my good and His glory. God used my darkest moment to relate to people of all walks of life who have experienced loss and help them overcome just like he helped me.

I definitely have so much more learning, unlearning, growing and healing to do. I've made mistakes, but I am committed to getting better, being better, and doing better. Who God calls us to be in every situation is one with a perspective of love. His way is better than our own understanding. The thing I've come to realize about life is, no matter where you are or what season you're walking through, you'll find yourself in spaces that require you to lead. The key to leadership is love.

Therefore, I want to make sure that as I go through life, my footprint leaves traces of love. So, what's next? With everything that I plan to accomplish next—graduating law school, becoming a new author, starting a law firm, scaling my fitness business and impacting more people—I am committed to figuring out what that looks like in my daily life and doing just that.

This is Briya 2.0.

About the Author

Briya Brown is a rising attorney, entrepreneur, author, and a fitness enthusiast located in the Washington metropolitan area. As a self-proclaimed servant of the people, Briya has dedicated her life to helping vulnerable communities by combatting health disparities, the wealth gap and promoting intergenerational mobility. Briya is also a trauma survivor, now using her truth to empower victims to exploit their pain for personal growth. Briya is currently a Juris Doctor Candidate at the University of Baltimore School of Law and is an active believer in Jesus. Find out more about Briya's work, book, and legacy at www.paintopowerbook.com.

Acknowledgments

Thank you God for your grace and mercy. By taking the time to truly cultivate my relationship with you, I was able to produce this.

My family and friends. My tribe. It really takes a village. Thank you for choosing me. Thank you for doing life with me and enduring tough times with me as we learn life together.

www.ingramcontent.com/pod-product-compliance
Lightning Source LLC
Chambersburg PA
CBHW022017290426
44109CB00015B/1206